I'll Know What To Do

A Kid's Guide To Natural Disasters

by

BONNIE S. MARK, Ph.D.

and

AVIVA LAYTON

illustrated by

Michael Chesworth

MAGINATION PRESS • Washington, DC

Library of Congress Cataloging-in-Publication Data

Mark, Bonnie S.
    I'll know what to do : a kid's guide to natural disasters / by
Bonnie S. Mark and Aviva Layton ; illustrated by Michael Chesworth.
        p.   cm.
    Includes bibliographical references (p.   -   ).
    Summary: Provides facts about earthquakes, hurricanes, tornadoes,
floods, and mud slides and discusses how to deal with and survive a
natural disaster.
    ISBN 1-55798-459-X
    1. Natural disasters—Juvenile literature. [1. Natural
disasters.]   I. Layton, Aviva. II. Chesworth, Michael, ill.
III. Title.
GB5019.M37   1997
155.9'35—dc21   96-51659
                                                                      CIP
                                                                       AC

Published by
MAGINATION PRESS
An Educational Publishing Foundation Book
American Psychological Association
750 First Street, NE
Washington, DC 20002

Manufactured in the United States of America

10 9 8 7 6 5 4 3 2

CONTENTS

FOREWORD
FOR PARENTS

Natural disasters evoke feelings of anxiety in all of us, but for children these feelings are intensified both by their own fears and by the fears of their parents. Some children keep their feelings inside. Other children act out their fears through their behavior.

In order for feelings of panic and anxiety to be resolved, these feelings must be identified, communicated, and understood. This gives the children a sense of control and the words for comprehending and addressing their experience. Communicating our feelings through words is an essential task that can be extremely challenging.

This book was written to assist children ages 8-13 to recover from traumas caused by natural disasters. The ideas developed are the result of extensive research and experience working with children, parents, and teachers, individually and in groups. Four fundamental concepts are discussed which have been found to facilitate healing: information, communication, reassurance, and the reestablishment of routine.

It is not unusual for children to take up to six months or more to resolve the trauma caused by stressors such as loss, accidents, crime, or natural disasters. This guidebook was written to help children respond to natural disasters in the most effective and healing ways.

1
DEALING WITH DISASTER

No matter where we live, no matter how careful we might be, Mother Nature has a habit of intruding on our lives. Tornadoes, earthquakes, hurricanes, fires, and floods can happen at any time, without much warning. When they do, they can send us on an emotional rollercoaster ride.

CHESWORTH

If you have ever lived through a natural disaster, you know that it doesn't feel "natural" at all. You might feel terrified one moment and brave the next, in control of the situation one moment and way out of control the next. You might feel angry with your parents because they can't protect you, and at the same time want them to take care of you.

How do you deal with all these different feelings? How can you make them work **for** you, not **against** you? This book offers some information to help guide you through the many feelings associated with a natural disaster.

If you have already experienced a natural disaster, this book will help you understand your feelings, and it will give you suggestions for what to do about them. If you are concerned about the possibility of a natural disaster happening in your area, the ideas and suggestions in this book will help you to feel less frightened and more in control. By reading this book, you are helping yourself, your friends, and your family know what to do about a natural disaster.

2
UNDERSTANDING THE FACTS

Learning about natural disasters can help you understand what has happened, or what can happen, so you will feel less afraid or anxious. Getting information is the most important thing that you can do to help yourself. This section answers questions such as: What are earthquakes? What causes floods? How do tornadoes and hurricanes develop? How fast do fires spread? It also gives some tips on how to prepare for each kind of disaster. You can find more information at your local library, at a bookstore, or by consulting the Resources section at the back of this book.

PREPARING FOR DISASTERS

Being prepared for any situation relieves a lot of the stress and fear. Knowing where to find things and having the **necessary supplies** on hand will make you and your family feel much safer in the event of an emergency. Here are some things your family should always have on hand:

flashlights
candles
a lighter
a first-aid kit
bottled water
a water purification kit
extra blankets
a battery-operated transistor radio
an extra supply of batteries

It is also a good idea to have a small portable kerosene stove for boiling water and heating canned food.

You can put all of these supplies in a big kitchen drawer or in a box by the front door. Or you can make an **emergency kit** in a plastic trash can with a tight lid. A large can with wheels is great for making a deluxe supply kit. You can place your supplies inside in layers. Start with the heavy water jugs and canned food on the bottom, then put in a layer of blankets and towels. Pack your first-aid supplies, a manual can opener, a radio, batteries, candles, a lighter, and matches on top of the blankets. If you like, you can include a few books or magazines, a toy, some money, and an extra set of car and house keys. Cover this layer with a set of clothes for each person in the family. A pair of socks, a change of underwear, and a sweatsuit or pants and a jacket should be enough. Include an umbrella or ponchos if you live in an area that is prone

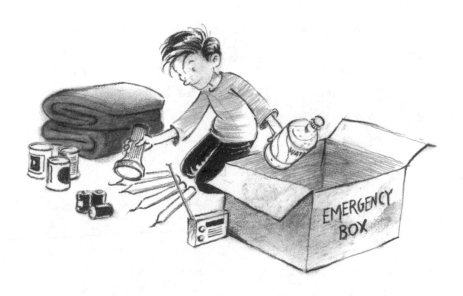

to rain and flooding. You should keep your emergency supply kit where you can find it quickly and easily. And you should check it every six months or so to make sure that everything inside is fresh and ready for use.

It's also very important to have a **family plan** in case something happens and you become separated. You could arrange to meet at a friend's place, school, a park, or any safe location your whole family can get to after an emergency. You can also arrange with a friend or family members who live in another town or state to be an information source. Because they live far away, they are not likely to be experiencing the natural disaster you are going through, so everyone in your family can call them to check in and get information about one another. Decide with your family what the best and safest plan is for you. Remember, though, it's always best to stay where you are during an emergency until it's safe to go to your meeting place.

These are general measures you can take to protect yourself in case of an emergency. Each disaster, however, has its own particular set of safety rules.

EARTHQUAKES

Nothing seems more solid or permanent to us than the ground we walk on. Yet the truth is, the earth is constantly in motion. This motion sometimes causes the sudden shaking of the ground we know as earthquakes.

Our earth is built in three layers. In the center, there is a <u>core</u>, which is made up of solid metal, mostly iron and nickel. The next layer is an extremely hot mass of molten metals and elements called the <u>mantle</u>. The outside layer, which we walk on, is called the <u>crust</u>, and it is very thin—only four to five miles deep. Because the crust is so thin, it has broken up into big chunks called <u>tectonic plates</u>. These plates float around on the liquid mantle underneath. This movement is called <u>tectonic drift</u>. Tectonic plates move very slowly—maybe a few inches a year—but they move constantly.

The breaks between the plates are called <u>faults</u>. When the plates rub against each other or bump into each other as they drift, they create the <u>shock waves</u>, or <u>seismic waves</u>, we call <u>earthquakes</u>. Plates meet in many different ways. Some brush against each other, going in different directions. Sometimes pieces of these plates catch on each

other, like a stuck zipper, and when they break loose, the earth shakes. Other plates bump up against each other, and cause quakes as one gets pushed under the other. This kind of movement pushes up mountain ranges and cliffs over millions of years.

Earthquakes happen all the time, everywhere. Although the strongest ones occur where large plates meet, such as California, Chile, Japan, and India, little ones that are too small to be felt happen every second, even in flat places like Kansas and Nebraska. The strength of earthquakes is measured on the <u>Richter scale</u>. Each move up the scale, which goes from 1.0 to 10.0, indicates a quake of ten times more power. Quakes measuring less than 3.1 are too weak to be felt by humans; quakes measuring over 8.1 only happen a few times each century.

Although separate earthquakes are happening all the time, large quakes at major pressure points sometimes come in a series. Quakes occurring before the main shock are called <u>preshocks</u>, and occur up to a month before the main earthquake. <u>Aftershocks</u> follow a quake, and continue for months or even years after the main earthquake is over.

Earthquakes also occur after volcanic eruptions, due to the pressure released by the lava flowing out of the earth. In the case of undersea earthquakes or volcanic eruptions, large waves call <u>tsunamis</u>, or <u>tidal waves</u>, occur as the shock waves roll through the ocean. These waves are the water equivalent of earthquakes, and can be hundreds of feet high when they reach the shore.

Seismology is the branch of science dedicated to studying earthquakes. Recent developments in satellite technology and sensitive shock-sensing devices have improved the ability of seismologists to track the earth's movements. They hope that one day we will be able to predict earthquakes.

Quick facts

* Two of the strongest quakes of the 20th century were the San Francisco earthquake of 1906 (8.1) and the Tokyo earthquake of 1924 (8.2).
* The 1993 Landers-Big Bear earthquake in California was still producing aftershocks two years after the initial tremor.
* Even in a flat place like Nebraska, there was a 3.4 earthquake in 1994.

What you can do to protect yourself from an earthquake

The best way to protect yourself from an earthquake is to take preventive measures. Chances are, the earth isn't going to crack open at your feet; that happens only in science-fiction movies. When people are injured in earthquakes, it is usually because things fall on them—things they could have protected themselves from with a little planning.

Check with your parents to make sure all heavy

objects such as pictures, bookcases, shelves, and mirrors are securely fastened so they don't fall down. Put special earthquake grips or sticky wax under vases, figures, or anything that might fly across the room or fall to the floor. Make sure that other heavy objects, like televisions, stereos, or computers, are stable on their desks or tables so that they don't slide or topple to the ground in a quake.

If you are outside when the earth starts shaking, move away from power lines or trees. Try to get into a clear space, like the center of a field or playground. If you are inside, crouch under a sturdy table or desk or stand in a doorway until the shaking stops. Always kneel down, wherever you are, and cover your neck and head with your arms to protect yourself in case anything does fall down around you.

FLOODS AND MUD SLIDES

When you water your lawn and forget to turn the sprinklers off, or leave the hose on too long, the water stops soaking into the ground and starts to pool up. The same thing happens with potted plants. If you pour too much water into the pot, it turns the soil to mud or drips out of the bottom. When you do any of these things, you are creating a miniature flood. Floods occur when the ground becomes supersaturated, meaning it cannot absorb any more water, or when there is too much water for the ground to absorb. The result is similar to putting a

plug into a bathtub or sink and then forgetting about it; because the water has nowhere to go, it rises and eventually overflows.

Floods can be caused by heavy rain, constant rain, rain on exceptionally dry ground, rain on frozen ground, or runoff from melting snow and ice. During the rainy seasons, so much rain can come down that the earth cannot absorb the water, so water flows across the land instead. Rivers break their banks and the water floods into the surrounding areas. In the Southwest and other desert areas, rain comes so infrequently that when it does, the dry earth may not be able to absorb it as quickly as it comes down. <u>Flash floods</u> can occur when water rushes into normally dry riverbeds at a very fast rate. Other

floods occur in the winter, when frozen ground cannot absorb water, or in the spring, when melting snow and ice cause rivers to overflow.

Floods can also be the result of other weather conditions, such as severe storms or hurricanes. Many cities and towns are situated on seacoasts, on shores of large lakes, or on riverbanks. When a storm strikes a seacoast at high tide, huge waves, known as storm surges, can wash over the town and cause floods. Other waves, called tsunamis, are caused by large underwater earthquakes or undersea volcano eruptions.

Mud slides can be even scarier than floods. They occur when rain softens the earth on the side of a mountain or hill and the whole mass comes loose. This can also happen when an earthquake strikes soon after a bad rainstorm. Generally, there is a warning that a mud slide could occur.

Quick facts

* Monsoon storms in India and southeast Asia cause great floods in those areas; over thousands of years, people have found ways to make the weather work for them by building rice paddies designed to catch flood waters.
* The biggest flood in history occurred on the Yellow River in China in October 1877.

What you can do to protect yourself in a flood or mud slide

Most civilizations have stories about floods that covered the whole earth and destroyed all but a few animals and plants. These stories make some people fear that this will happen today. In actuality, there is little to worry about because floods today always dry out fairly soon.

Though floods can be very destructive, except for flash floods, they are one of the few natural disasters that we can predict and plan for, even if we can't stop them. The best way to stay safe in a flood is to get out of the water's reach. Make sure you know the quickest route to high ground, and go there as soon as you can after you get a flood warning. Take food and warm clothes with you, and whatever valuables you can carry.

You and your family should decide together what is most important to save from the floodwaters. Most likely these will be things that are irreplaceable—family photographs, small paintings, favorite books and toys, or special letters. Make sure your pet is close by so that it doesn't get left behind when the rest of the family moves to high ground. If you have enough advance notice, sandbag your house and garage to help prevent water from getting inside.

Floods can come slowly or quickly. Sometimes, you can watch the water level rise inch by inch. With flash floods, however, there is no warning, and the water comes rushing down the riverbed at a speed so fast it washes away anything in its path. So be sure you never build a campsite in a dry riverbed—a storm can come without any warning at any time!

If a mud slide is predicted in your area, follow the same procedures that you would in a flood. Usually it is people living on or near mountains, cliffs, beaches, or riverbanks who are threatened by mud slides. It's important that you move out of harm's way as soon as you can after getting a mud slide warning. Slides are much less predictable than floods, and act like avalanches. Loose mud moves faster than you can, so pack your things quickly, grab your pets, and go.

HURRICANES

Hurricanes are massive rainstorms that develop over the warm, humid seas of the tropics. Warm air rises, and

in the tropical oceans, the air also carries a lot of evaporated moisture, which develops into rain clouds. An area of low air pressure, called a <u>tropical depression,</u> can turn into a hurricane if the warm air is replaced by cooler air fast enough. Hurricanes usually develop between July and October, and may last up to 30 days. They get their energy from warm tropical ocean water and weaken as they move toward colder northern ocean waters or inland, away from the ocean.

Hurricanes grow in a spiral pattern around a calm center, called the <u>eye of the storm</u>, and their winds blow outward. The winds always blow away from the Equator, so in the Northern Hemisphere, hurricanes spin counterclockwise, while in the Southern Hemisphere they turn clockwise. The eye of a hurricane is a completely calm, windless region, about 20 miles wide. Because the power of the storm moves outward from the center, the <u>wall clouds</u> surrounding the eye are the most powerful part of the storm. Inside the wall clouds, winds blow up to 150 miles per hour. The winds of a hurricane cover an area of about 500 miles (800 kilometers), and their force can topple trees, blow off roofs, and hurl cars from the road. Hurricanes bring heavy rainstorms, gusting winds, and storm surge waves with them, and the deluge of water usually causes some flooding. As they move in from the ocean, they slow down and fade into rainstorms, because they depend on the upward flow of warm ocean air for their energy.

Tropical storms with winds over 75 mph that form over the western Pacific Oceans are called <u>typhoons</u>, while storms that form over the Indian Ocean and its seas are called cyclones.

Quick facts

* Recent hurricanes that hit the Atlantic coast of the United States include Hugo (1989), Andrew (1991), and Bertha (1996).
* Hurricanes are named according to charts that run in six-year cycles. The names go through the letters of the alphabet and alternate male names and female names. Names of particularly notable storms are removed from the list.

What you can do to protect yourself from a hurricane

Thanks to sophisticated satellite and radar tracking of hurricanes and tropical storms, we always have advance warning of their arrival. Listen to TV and radio news for information. If you are told to evacuate your area and move inland, do so immediately. Be sure to take your supplies and valuables with you. If you have time, board up your windows and sandbag your house before you go. Boarding up your windows or putting tape on them can prevent them from being shattered by the strong hurricane winds, and placing sandbags around your house can help protect it from possible floods.

If it's safe to stay in your house, stay away from windows and don't go outside until the hurricane is over. It is a good idea to fill your bathtubs with water, and make sure you have fresh batteries for radios and flashlights, in case the electricity goes out during the storm. Have candles and matches or a lighter handy as well.

If you can't get inside during the storm, stay away from trees, cars, and plate glass windows. The safest thing you can do is lie down and cover your head and neck with your hands.

Remember that hurricanes have eyes, or calm areas. The eye of a storm can be very wide, and sometimes people think that the storm is over while the eye is passing overhead. Because the most dangerous part of the storm surrounds the eye, it's very important that you stay inside until you're told it's safe to go out—even if the winds stops blowing and the rain stops pouring down outside. Hurricanes rarely just stop; they taper off. When the hurricane has passed, a rainstorm will usually follow.

TORNADOES

Tornadoes, or twisters, are the most powerful storms on earth. They are destructive, whirling windstorms that grow out of thunderclouds. Like hurricanes, they depend on areas of low pressure and on rising warm air for their energy. However, they are the exact opposite of hurricanes in that their winds spin inward, creating funnel-shaped clouds.

In the United States, tornadoes usually occur in the mid-

western states in the late spring and early summer. They are especially common in Texas, Oklahoma, Missouri, Kansas, and Nebraska. When a low-pressure front develops, warm air rises into a cloud mass and begins to spin, creating an inward spiral. As warm air gets sucked into the spiral, more air rushes in to replace it, creating a constant flow upward into the <u>thunderhead</u>, which eventually grows into the funnel-shaped twister of the tornado. The winds of a tornado spin counterclockwise in the Northern Hemisphere and clockwise in the Southern Hemisphere, and blow at speeds of up to 300 miles per hour.

Most tornadoes never <u>strike</u>, or touch, the ground. Those that do are the most dangerous, but even airborne tornadoes can cause terrible damage as they pass over buildings and roads. Tornadoes last from one to three hours and usually travel between 20 and 200 miles. The bottom of a tornado that strikes is usually fairly narrow, but airborne tornadoes can be up to a mile wide.

The updraft of a tornado's winds is exceptionally powerful; it acts like a vacuum, sucking air up into the storm. This vacuum suction can pull roofs off buildings, toss cars and animals hundreds of feet, and uproot trees and plants.

Quick facts

* The fastest tornado recorded struck on March 18, 1925, in Missouri, and traveled over 220 miles at 60 miles per hour.
* Tornadoes have been known to pick up objects, such as desks, and deposit them unharmed miles from where they originated.

What you can do to protect yourself from a tornado

Tornadoes are very unpredictable, but you can usually spot them before they strike the ground. Very large tor-

nadoes are strong enough to pick up animals, people, or cars, so try to stay inside.

If you are outside when a tornado hits, lie face down and cover your head with your hands, just as you would in a hurricane. Stay as low and flat on the ground as you can to protect yourself from the wind.

If you are inside, move to the middle of the first floor, or into a basement or cellar, if possible. Tornadoes have very low air pressure at the center of the funnel, so when they pass over buildings, the pressure outside is lower than the pressure inside. As a result, buildings or houses that get "hit" by tornadoes sometimes explode, because the outside air pressure is not great enough to hold the walls or windows against the inside pressure. Stay away from windows that might shatter or doors that might blow off their hinges. Tornadoes can also pull the roofs off buildings, which is why a basement or cellar is the safest place. Some people also recommend lying in a bathtub with a mattress on top of you.

FIRES

Wildfires

Wildfires can start in many different ways. Their frequency and severity vary according to location, weather, and kind of vegetation. Fires usually happen in the late summer and fall, when the ground and plants are dry from months of heat and lack of rain. Dead, dry brush or grasses catch fire very easily and burn rapidly, allowing wildfires to spread very quickly. Hot, dry, windy weather or drought conditions contribute to the chances of fires starting, and to their destructiveness. Fires usually start when people are careless with matches, cigarettes, or campfires, but in extremely dry weather fires can start by themselves in the underbrush or when lightning strikes dry trees. Wildfires can last for days, weeks, or months, depending on the vegetation and the weather conditions.

Forestry agencies in each state are responsible for training firefighters and for providing public education about fire safety. Two methods of putting out fires are used to combat forest fires and brush fires. A <u>direct attack</u> involves smothering the fire with water or other retardants dropped from helicopters or sprayed from hoses, or throwing dirt or sand on burning vegetation. An <u>indirect attack</u> involves creating <u>firebreaks</u> by clearing out brush and vegetation to starve the fire of fuel.

Even though wildfires seem highly destructive, they do serve a purpose in nature. Every time a fire burns through a forest or across mountains, it rids the land of dead vegetation and opens up space for new trees and

plants to grow. Fires, even ones that are started by people, are part of the cycle of the forest and of its constant regeneration.

House fires

Fires can start in people's homes for a number of reasons. Usually, house fires start because of carelessness. Some are caused by neglect of things like burning candles, matches, or cigarettes. If these items are not completely doused, they can start fires when dropped in trash cans. Carelessness with fireplace ashes can also start fires, either in the house, as a result of sparks, or in garbage containers, when people throw out ashes that are still "alive."

Kitchen fires are a fairly common occurrence. When a stove is left on, but not lit, flammable gas escapes into the air, and any spark can cause a fire to start. Broilers, malfunctioning toasters, and irons can also cause fires when not watched closely. Fires can also be started when sparks from exposed electrical outlets or frayed electrical cords land on flammable materials, like carpeting or wood. Trees and bushes close to the house can also catch fire if they are not regularly trimmed. And in an area prone to brush fires, overgrown backyard plants can attract wildfires to your home.

Quick facts

✳ The largest recorded forest fire burned 13,500 square miles on the island of Borneo from February to June 1983.

* Forest and brush fires can burn as fast as five miles per hour.
* The Yellowstone National Forest had completely re-generated by 1995, only seven years after the devastating fires of July and August 1988.

What you can do to protect yourself from a fire

Fires can move very quickly through an apartment or house. Always have a fire extinguisher on hand and know how to use it—once a fire starts, you won't have time to read the instructions. Make a plan with your family so that everyone knows the fastest, safest route out of every room. If you have security bars or screens on your doors or windows, make sure you know how to release them for easy escape. If you get caught in your house, drop down to the floor and crawl out on your stomach. Smoke and heat rise, so the closer you stay to the ground, the fresher the air will be and the better you'll be able to see your way out. If you are outside, run as fast as you can to get away from the fire. If your clothing catches fire, stop running, drop to the ground, and roll over and over to smother the flames.

To prevent house fires from happening, always be very careful with matches, candles, fireplace ashes, or cigarettes. Douse them with water before throwing them into trashcans to make sure they are completely out. Fires sometimes start because of gas leaks, so it's important to have your pipes checked every once in a while. If you are going on a long vacation, have your gas turned off to prevent a leak while you are gone. If you smell gas in your house, turn off the gas main and call the gas company to come and check your house. Fires can be caused by faulty electric wiring, so watch out for exposed, sparking, or fraying wires, exposed sockets, or liquid near electric outlets. Have anything that looks dangerous repaired immediately. Again, if you are leaving on vacation, unplug appliances like irons, toasters, and laundry dryers to prevent fires from starting while you are away.

When you first move into a house or apartment, it should be thoroughly inspected to help ensure that it is safe. You and your parents should also do some checking before you go to sleep or leave the house. It is important that you discuss with your parents how you can make your home safe from fire.

In the case of forest fires or wildfires, you usually have time to prepare. You, your family, and your neighbors can listen to news reports to learn how close the fire is to your area. Since fires are unpredictable, it is best that you get ready ahead of time so that you can leave quickly should a fire head your way. Pack things that are important to you so that you will have them when you need them, and remember to take your pets. If you have time and the firefighters aren't using the hydrants on your street, it's a good idea to water down the roof of your house and to water the ground around the house to help prevent the house from catching fire.

3

HOW YOU FEEL

FEARFUL FEELINGS

Fear is a natural reaction to any danger that threatens your safety. It's scary when winds threaten to blow off your roof. It's scary when water floods your house. It's scary when the ground below your feet starts shaking. You may look to adults for reassurance, but what happens when they are so busy responding to the crisis that they don't have time for you? A natural disaster can be a frightening time for everyone, no matter what age you are.

After a disaster, you may feel afraid of a lot of things. You may be scared of being separated from your family or of being left alone. You may be worried about the disaster happening again. Even after all danger has passed, your imagination may still work overtime. Even if you are not easily scared, you may now feel fearful. You may feel helpless and unable to do anything about what is happening. Remember, whatever you are feeling is OK. No one is too old to feel scared!

"GROWN-UP" FEELINGS

Sometimes disasters make us act in a competent and mature way. There may be moments during and after a disaster when you feel very "grown-up." Sisters and brothers who fight constantly often get along—at least for a while. Instead of wanting to tease your brothers or sisters, you may want to protect or comfort them. You will probably want to help your parents in whatever way you can. The next section of this book suggests different ways to help.

"LITTLE KID" FEELINGS

Sometimes disasters can make us act younger than we are. Instead of feeling like an adult, you feel like a little kid again. Don't worry—this is normal. During or after a natural disaster, you may wish for someone to take care of you. You may feel angry, confused, sad, or very young and alone. These are all normal reactions, which can occur even up to six months, or more, after a scary experience. For example, before the disaster, you may have felt very independent. Afterward, you may want to be with your parents as much as possible. You may find that separating is difficult. Some kids feel scared to go to school or don't want to go out. Some kids feel deserted whenever they are left alone. Some kids feel jumpy. Some kids start to misbehave. Almost everyone, including adults, has trouble sleeping at night.

SLEEP PROBLEMS

After a natural disaster, you may experience some sleep problems, even if you have never had them before. You may not be able to fall asleep. When you do fall asleep, you might be woken up by nightmares. One reason is that at bedtime, when everything is quiet, you can remember the shock of what has happened. You may have been so busy doing things all day long that you didn't have time to think, but at night memories come back to make you feel afraid again.

When we are drifting off to sleep or dreaming, fears can be exaggerated. You may feel frightened of being swallowed up by the earth, eaten by fire, washed away by floods, or blown away by winds. Fear of separation from parents and worries that you will be left alone are also normal feelings that can keep you awake at night. You might even notice that your mother or father seems scared too, and that could make you even more scared. **Everyone needs to feel safe!**

Changes in your bedtime routines can also affect you. Most families have special things they do before going to sleep. You may take a bath, brush your teeth, put on pajamas, listen to music, read stories, or watch a video or television. Doing the same thing each night can help us feel safe, comfortable, and protected. But if the disaster has disrupted the things you usually do, you may feel insecure. Even if you never thought about your routines before, you may now find yourself really missing them.

There are other things that can be upsetting at night, too. Maybe the person who usually says goodnight is not there. Of course, this can happen when your parents are sick or go on vacation, but it is much more upsetting when it happens because of a disaster. Or you may be scared of the dark. Lots of people are, including adults, and the dark becomes even scarier during or after a disaster.

OUT-OF-CONTROL FEELINGS

After a natural disaster, bedtime routines aren't the only ones to be disrupted. All your normal schedules are turned upside down, and just about everyone feels helpless and unhappy about these changes. Even if you hate getting up for classes, for instance, you may feel sad if school closes unexpectedly. You may feel that if only you could get to your soccer practice, or art class, or go to your friend's home to play, everything would be better. We all have these types of feelings because we like to feel in control of our lives. Both adults and kids like to be able to predict what's going to happen in the coming minutes, hours, and days. You plan for vacations, plan for schoolwork, plan for after-school activities, and when you have to alter these plans, all kinds of feelings arise. Sometimes you feel annoyed or resentful. Sometimes you feel relief that you don't have to practice the piano or do your homework. Whatever your feelings, trying to understand them and talking about them are two things that can help you feel better.

OTHER FEELINGS

Although you may feel **relief** that you and your family are OK, you may also feel **guilty** that others were not as lucky as you were. You may feel **proud** that you handled yourself well, or **ashamed** that you panicked during the crisis. You many feel **excited** that something so interesting is happening. You may feel **close** to others who have lived through a disaster with you, even if you were not especially close to them before. You may feel **grateful** to those who helped. You may feel a combination of all these feelings, but don't worry—all of us experience these feelings after a disaster.

4

WHAT YOU CAN DO

GAINING CONTROL

It's hard for you to feel <u>in</u> control when nature goes <u>out</u> of control, but there are things you can do to help yourself. You can try to be as calm as possible. You can cooperate by following instructions and going to the safest location. The best thing you can do, though, is to be prepared before a disaster happens. With some disasters—like tornadoes and hurricanes—you usually have some warning, but other disasters—like earthquakes and fires—can happen suddenly. Preparing ahead can really help you gain control. Later in this section we will suggest steps you can take to prepare yourself.

GETTING INFORMATION

Both during and after the disaster, one of the best ways you can feel safe is to understand what has happened and what is happening now. This can start with something as basic as knowing where the important

people in your life are. Even if the adults around you are very busy, it helps to know what they are doing and where they can be found. Let your family know that you need information and reassurance.

Asking questions is very helpful, and it's always OK, even if you are feeling afraid or embarrassed. It is very important to know as much as you can, and the best way to get answers is to ask! Adults want to protect you, so sometimes they may not tell you what is happening because they don't want to frighten you. When you ask questions, it helps them know what your concerns are. If you have a hard time asking specific questions, let them know that you are really worried, confused, curious, or frightened, and ask them to try to help you.

YOUR OWN EMERGENCY KIT

Even if your parents seem to be prepared, one of the ways for you to feel better about a natural disaster is for you to prepare, too! For example, knowing where your own flashlight is (with an extra set of batteries taped to it) can make a big difference. You can prepare an emergency kit. Your emergency kit can be packed in a suitcase, box, duffle bag, or backpack that is not being used for anything else. It can also be packed in a plastic trashcan—large or small—with a lid that fits securely. Inside your container you can put a change of clothes, a pair of shoes, your own bottled water, bandaids, some protein bars, even your favorite chocolate bar. You can add some books, a pad of paper and drawing pens, or a favorite game or toy. Talk with your family about what kinds of things you should add to your emergency kit based on the types of disasters you are likely to encounter. Being physically ready helps you become mentally ready.

YOUR ROOM

Make sure your room is safe so that nothing can fall and hurt you. Put a pair of sneakers beside the bed and keep your emergency kit where you can get to it quickly. It's always comforting, no matter how old you are, to have your favorite toy or stuffed animal nearby. Know where your flashlight is, and be sure you know the fastest way out of your room. You and your family should know

how to release security bars or punch out screens, should it become necessary.

PRACTICE DRILLS

You should also practice emergency routines and know how to work the windows and the door locks. Make sure you know where to find the ladder or the fire escape, especially if you are not living or sleeping on the ground floor. One of the most important things you can do with your family is to plan a central meeting place so that everyone knows where to go.

Emergency practice drills can help the whole family know how to react during a natural disaster. These drills will help you to learn how you and your family can keep safe, and they will help you feel more in control. Most important, be sure you and your family talk, plan, and share information before, during, and after a natural disaster.

TALKING

Putting feelings into words and communicating with others are very important parts of healing. When something really bad or scary happens, it helps to share your experiences and feelings. It's the same for adults. After a trauma, neighbors start to get to know one another better and communities look toward others for assistance. We all come together to fight our common enemy—fear.

From all over the city or state, newscasters ask people, "What's it like where you are?" "What does it feel like to you?" There is comfort and safety in knowing what it's

like for other people. By talking and exchanging information, you can learn you are not alone and that others share your feelings of fear, excitement, helplessness, worry, and anticipation of things to come. By sharing your feelings, you can also help others recognize and understand their own.

You may find that the same thing happens among your friends. For example, when something really bad happens while you're at school, even the class bully quiets down and wants to get along. This is because the "coming together" of people helps to make it safer for everyone. Often we don't understand our feelings until we share them with others. That's why you should never keep your feelings bottled up inside. Don't be embarrassed to say, "I just don't know what I am feeling" or "I'm feeling really scared."

RELAXING

During and after a natural disaster, things may seem so confusing that you may not know where to begin. One place to start is to take some deep breaths. Taking deep, slow breaths helps you gain control over your body. You can then help yourself relax by doing the following exercise. As you inhale, count from 1 to 5. Next, hold your breath for a second or two. Slowly exhale, and slowly say the word "relax" out loud to yourself. You may want to practice this exercise or ask your parents to help you to remember it.

HELPING

There are many ways you can help during and after a natural disaster. You can help with brothers and sisters and with neighbors. You can visit the elderly or comfort small children. You can also check out the neighborhood with your parents, and report potential dangers, such as falling debris or cracks in walls. It is very important that you keep calm and notice what's going on around you. It also helps to think about others and how you can keep them safe or make them feel better.

All of these activities can help you feel better, both at the time of the disaster and long after the disaster has passed. Your fear may not be about what has just happened, but that it might happen again. That is why it is important to try to recognize and understand all your feelings.

ACTIVITIES

Here is a list of things you can do to help you understand how the natural disaster has affected you and your community.

* **Make an album.** Take photographs or clip out newspaper photos and articles. Put them into an album you buy, or make your own from colored paper. You might want to add captions for your photos. Write something about what happened to you, your family, and friends, and add it to your album.

* **Make art.** Draw, color, paint, or do other artwork. Through your art, you can express and learn about your feelings.

* **Write a script** for a movie or play. Create and act out a part. The stories can be anything from family histories to action dramas to disaster plots to horror stories. Writing and acting put you in charge. *You* can control the outcome of your story.

* **Write stories, poems, or newspaper articles** from your point of view. After the Los Angeles earthquake, some teenagers got together and wrote a series of articles for their school paper entitled *January 17, 1994—LA Rocks*.

* **Write letters** to friends, relatives, teachers, or pen pals. Writing about what happened can help you to understand it better.

* If you have a computer, **communicate through e-mail,** both with kids who experienced the disaster and with others who live farther away. Tell them what you have gone through, and learn about their experiences.

* If you have access to a video recorder, **make your own videotape** of the reactions of your friends, family, and community to the disaster.

* **Map out your house or apartment** so you know where everything is and where to go in case of a disaster.

* **Do practice drills** with your family so that you will be ready in case of another emergency.

* **Do the "complete-a-thought" exercise** on the following pages.

COMPLETE-A-THOUGHT EXERCISE
(FILL IN THE BLANKS)

When I think about the **earthquake, flood, hurricane, tornado, fire** *(circle one)*, my feelings are _____
_____
_____
_____
_____

The most important thing I learned about the **earthquake, flood, hurricane, tornado, fire** *(circle one),* is _____
_____
_____
_____
_____

If a little kid asked me about **earthquake, flood, hurricane, tornado, fire** *(circle one),* I would say _____
_____
_____
_____
_____

If we have another **earthquake, flood, hurricane, tornado, fire** *(circle one),* I hope _____
_____
_____
_____
_____

Complete-a-Thought Exercise *(continued)*

My biggest fears are _____
_____
_____
_____
_____

What I am doing to combat my worry is _____
_____
_____
_____
_____

What I do before I go to sleep is _____
_____
_____
_____
_____

Some of the things that interrupt my falling asleep or sleeping through the night are _____
_____
_____
_____
_____

What I can do to help myself feel better is _____
_____
_____
_____
_____

Complete-a-Thought Exercise *(continued)*

A natural disaster can really make you think about your life, your attitudes, your values, and your plans.

The most important things in life to me at this time are _____

_____

_____

_____

_____

If I had only one minute to gather my most important things, I would take _____

_____

_____

_____

_____

What I would like to happen in my life in the next year or two is

_____

_____

_____

_____

_____

If you wish, you can write these out on another sheet of paper, so you have plenty of room to include all of your ideas.

Remember, there are no right or wrong answers!

NEWSPAPER CLIPPING AND PHOTO PAGES

Take photographs or cut out newspaper photos and articles, and paste them on these pages.

WRITING PAGES

These pages are for you to write letters, poems, stories, or movie scripts about your experiences. These stories don't have to be real. They can come from deep within your imagination.

_____

_____

_____

_____

_____

_____

_____

_____

_____

_____

_____

_____

_____

_____

_____

_____

_____

5
CONCLUSION

All of us have different reactions to natural disasters. Nightmares, sleeplessness, fear, anger, anxiety, and even "spaciness" are common responses for people of all ages. In fact, it would be unnatural **not** to feel at least one of these. So whatever you're feeling, you are definitely not alone.

The most important thing you can do is to talk about your feelings with your friends and family. Sharing your

feelings about the experience and asking questions can help you and others to feel better. Also, remember that things always get better. It just may take a little time.

Mother Nature is unpredictable, but being prepared for natural disasters makes them much less frightening. Make a plan with your family about what to do in case a disaster occurs. Make emergency kits. Learn about disasters, how they work and why they happen. In fact, by reading this book you have already started to be prepared!

While Mother Nature may have some frightening surprises in store, she has many more delights. Prepare for the disasters, but always remember to enjoy sunny days, puffy clouds, gentle breezes, sweet-smelling flowers, colorful sunsets, and soft snowflakes.

RESOURCES

FICTION STORIES

Earthquakes

Cottonwood, Joe. *Quake: A Novel.* New York, Scholastic Press, 1995. With their parents trapped at the World Series baseball game in Candlestick Part, 14-year-old Franny, her younger brother, and their cousin brave the aftermath of the 1989 Loma Prieta earthquake alone.

Gregory, Kristiana. *Earthquake at Dawn.* New York, Harcourt Brace, 1992. A fictionalized account of photographer Edith Irvine's experience in San Francisco immediately after the great 1906 earthquake, based on the letters of survivors and on Irvine's photographs of the destroyed city.

Kudlinski, Kathleen. *Earthquake.* New York, Puffin Books, 1993. A view of the 1906 San Francisco earthquake and the great fire that ruined the city, as told by a young boy living there with his family.

Lowell, Susan. *I Am Lavina Cumming.* Minneapolis, MN, Milkweed Editions, 1993. While living with relatives in San Francisco after the death of her mother, 10-year-old Lavina Cumming faces the 1906 San Francisco earthquake and Great Fire.

Fires

Williams, Vera. *A Chair for My Mother.* New York, Morrow, 1982. An illustrated story about a girl who, with her mother and grandmother, saves dimes and quarters to buy new furniture after all the family belongings are lost in a house fire.

Floods

Burton, Hester. *Flood at Reedsmere.* Cleveland, World Publishing Co., 1968. A sophisticated story by Carnegie Medal winner Burton about a pair of friends, Mark and Mary, and their adventures rescuing their neighbors after a flood hits their small British town.

Cousins, Lucy. *Noah's Ark.* Cambridge, MA, Candlewick Press, 1993. A very simple, illustrated story about the Flood and Noah's ark, written by the author of the Maisy the Mouse series of books.

Gross, Virginia T. *The Day It Rained Forever.* New York, Viking, 1991. The story of the famous Johnstown flood, told through the eyes of a young girl who watches her town disappear after a nearby dam gives way in a storm.

Locker, Thomas. *The Boy Who Held Back The Sea.* New York, Dial Books, 1987. A beautifully illustrated account of a young boy who saves his own town from flooding by blocking a leaking hole in a dike.

Hurricanes

Cole, Joanna. *The Magic School Bus: Inside the Eye of a Hurricane.* New York, Scholastic Press, 1995. With this activity and picture book, the Magic School Bus series takes Ms. Frizzle's class—and readers—inside the eye of a hurricane.

Dorris, Michael. *Morning Girl.* New York, Hyperion Books, 1992. The story of a brother and sister, Star Boy and Morning Girl, who help their tribe through a hurricane and the arrival of European settlers to their Caribbean island.

Weeks, Sarah. *Hurricane City.* New York, HarperCollins, 1993. This illustrated book makes a rhyming poem out of the alphabetical names of hurricanes, and describes the effects of each on a town in which hurricane season is never over.

Wiesner, David. *Hurricane.* New York, Colarion Books, 1990. The morning after a hurricane strikes their town, two brothers find that an uprooted tree suddenly has the magical power to transport them wherever they can imagine going.

NONFICTION BOOKS

Running Press Discovery Kits. *The Weather Tracker's Kit: Explore the Changing Forces of Nature.* A wonderful activity kit that allows kids to be meteorologists. Includes an 80-page book describing different weather patterns—from the various cloud formations to how hurricanes form—and a weather forecasting kit complete with a meteorological log and a list of international weather symbols.

Allaby, Michael. Reader's Digest: *How the Weather Works.* New York, Dorling Kindersley, 1995. A sophisticated children's encyclopedia of the weather. Using diagrams and photographs, the book defines all kinds of weather patterns, including global climates, weather fronts, and urban weather conditions. User—friendly activities and experiments accompany each different unit.

Armbruster, Ann, and Taylor, Elizabeth. *Tornadoes.* New York, Franklin Watts, 1989. An overview of the scientific anatomy of tornadoes that includes home experiments and activities to enhance understanding of the material. The book also includes a section on government agencies and weather bureaus that track tornadoes and issue storm warnings.

Craig, M. J. *Questions and Answers About the Weather.* New York, Scholastic, 1996. A newly illustrated reissue of Craig's 1969 guide to the 50 most commonly asked questions about the weather, from why lightning zigzags or flashes to how the wind blows.

Curtis, Neil, and Allaby, Michael. *Visual Factfinder: Planet Earth*. New York, Kingfisher Books, 1993. An excellent general encyclopedia of the planet. Bright graphics, diagrams, and photographs accompany the sections covering the earth's climates, basic geology, land formations, weather patterns, and topographical features.

Erlbach, Arlene. *Tornadoes!* Chicago, Children's Press, 1994. A simple 50-page illustrated reader covering the why and how of tornadoes, safety concerns and precautions in tornado conditions, explanations of forecasting methods, and a glossary of related terms.

Lampton, Christopher. *Disaster: Blizzard, Earthquake, Forest Fire, Hurricane, Tornado, Volcano*. Brookfield, CT, Millbrook Press, 1991. A moderately advanced series that blends famous examples of each type of natural disaster with scientific explanations, descriptions of prediction and measurement technologies, and helpful glossaries of related terms.

Lauber, Patricia. *Hurricanes: Earth's Mightiest Storms*. New York, Scholastic, 1996. A sophisticated book that gives a global lesson in hurricanes. Explains the natural causes of hurricanes, describes the new satellite tracking methods, gives examples of famous storms, and includes a section on the different types of hurricanes that occur around the world.

Lee, Sally. *Hurricanes*. New York, Franklin Watts, 1993. This advanced book uses detailed scientific descriptions, understandable graphics and diagrams, and easy home activities to explain the meteorological background of hurricanes and to describe basic home preparedness in storm conditions.

Simon, Seymour. Mulberry Books: *Wildfires*. New York, Morrow, 1996. This easy reader, while stressing the danger of wildfires and describing safety precautions, also explains fires in the context of the natural cycle of the forest. The overriding message is one of reassurance, and Simon uses the 1988 Yellowstone fires to illustrate the regenerative capabilities of the wilderness.

Souza, D. M. *Hurricanes*. Minneapolis, Carolrhoda Books, 1996. A fairly advanced book that describes the basics of hurricane forecasting, storm formation, and interesting facts. The book is filled with photographs of recent hurricanes and has a wonderful section on preparedness and on reacting to storm warnings.

Van Cleave, Janice. *Earthquakes*. New York, John Wiley & Sons, 1993. A wonderful activity book that seeks to teach the scientific principles behind earthquakes and plate tectonics through easy, fun home experiments. Also includes reading projects and other activities.

Vogel, Carole G. *Shock Waves Through Los Angeles: The Northridge Earthquake*. New York, Little, Brown, 1996. An excellent book that combines factual reportage, photographs, and scientific data to explain the 1994 Northridge earthquake. Includes discussions of cutting—edge seismological theories such as thrust faults and strike-slip faults to explain the impact of the quake and the seismic future of the Los Angeles Basin.

Afterword

This book combines the insights and collective wisdom of many people who came together in order to help heal the families in our community following an earthquake in Los Angeles. We are very appreciative of Charlotte Gusay, a woman of many talents, for her tireless dedication to the project; Allison Hoffman, an extraordinarily brilliant and creative assistant; and Mary Rafferty, for her innovative and persistent support at every stage. We are also indebted to the following remarkable people who assisted in various ways with this project: Matthew and Marion Solomon, James Incorvaia, Donald Tessmer, Loren Judaken, Mayume Hattori, Velveth Dardon, Lili Bosse, Ashley and Lauren Berger, Daniel and Benji Reiss, and Jeff Blume. Finally, a very special thank you to Ariel Mark for his curiosity, for asking the right questions, and for expressing the feelings that inspired this book.

Bonnie S. Mark and Aviva Layton
July 1997

"Since we cannot change Reality,
let us change the eyes which see reality."
—Nikos Kazantzakis